Journey Inward
Reflections for Your
Spiritual Growth and Peace of Mind

Margi Lantos-Chastain

Spiritual Bridges Books
Portland, Oregon

Spiritual Bridges Books

Copyright © 2003 by Margi Lantos-Chastain
All Rights Reserved. No part of this book may be used or reproduced in any form without written permission from the author.

First Printing May, 2003

First Edition

ISBN: 0-9728237-1-9

Printer:
Lithtex Printing - www.lithtex.com

Spiritual Bridges World Wide Website Address is:
www.spiritualbridges.com

Telephone: 503.722.8631
P.O. Box 2367 Clackamas, OR 97015
E-mail: please see website for new address

This book is dedicated to my family
for the support you've given me,
to my friends
for your encouragement,
to my clients for making this book possible,
and to my beautiful Angels
for endless miracles.

*You are always loved, wherever you go
and whatever you do . . .*

Foreword

Being grateful simply opens doors to endless possibilities...

Late one evening, as I was thanking the Universe for monetary gifts I had just received, a subtle thought slowly slipped into my mind: "Why not write a book in which I can simply ask a question, be gently guided to a page, and receive a comforting answer?" In that moment I knew (as I was truly being grateful) that I had created a reward along with a gift — a gift of writing a book, a book not only for myself but for all to use.

So the journey began. That night my Divine guidance (Angels, Spirit Guides, Higher-Self, God) guided my writing. Endless reflections just flowed from my mind. It was as if I was linked with Divine love and the vast array of energy coming from it. The love not only felt very real, but it also allowed me to feel more alive than I have ever felt.

As the writing that evening came to a close, a soft whisper gently acknowledged that more will be written and all in good time....

I am sincerely honored to gift to you these gentle messages that have come from a Higher source — to guide you on your journey, to protect your heart, and to most humbly comfort you in times of need, great or small. Enjoy!

I have been directed to provide a few methods on how to use this book:

Start by asking the Universe for protection:
1. Visualize a white light of love streaming from heaven moving through and around you.

2. Ask for the highest and finest vibrations of love to envelop you.

Follow any method you feel compelled to use:
1. As you ask a question for yourself or someone else, choose one of these methods:

   - Gently guide yourself to a page and read it.

   - Visualize or pick a number from 8-320 and read what is on that page.

   - Place yourself in a quiet meditative state and allow your fingers to gently move over the pages, listening for an internal voice tell you when to stop. Read that page.

2. Don't ask a question, but use one of the methods just mentioned. Be open to the guidance you receive or need at that moment.

3. Read a page daily in consecutive order.

4. Create your own method.

Here are a few questions and ideas I use:

> "My beautiful (Angels, Spirit Guides, Higher-Self, God, etc.), please guide me wherever I need to go."
>
> "What do I need to know at this time?"
>
> "Divine guidance, direct me."
>
> "What will I need to benefit from today?"
>
> "What message do you have for me?"

I so hope you enjoy this book as much as I enjoyed writing it. Please feel free to carry it with you as a soul companion on your inward spiritual journey. I pray that you never feel alone again.

Many beautiful blessings are sent your way!

Love,
  Margi

Be still and listen to the beating of your heart...what is it whispering to you?

Forgiveness is the Universe
rewarding you with peace…
whom do you have to forgive?

The present moment seeks only now...
take it all in...breathe...

Your angels are with you…
holding you…
let go, let God, release and live…

To understand is to be free…
to let go is to live…
how are you going to live life
from this moment on?

*Do you hear the inner whispers
guiding you? Listen, listen…
what are they saying to you?*

*The inner child is calling you…
go out and play…*

Smile…
the Universe has just taken your
picture…let your spirit soar,
you beautiful soul!

Today is just another ordinary day, or is it? Why not make it extraordinary and do something for someone… give back to your world…

Angels say:
"We understand how you're feeling...
because many times we have carried
that pain for you...now once again...
release and surrender it to us...
we love you..."

Isn't it a beautiful day? If not,
well, then why not make it one…

If the rains hadn't come...
we would have all dried up...

Blessed be the little ones...
for they are the lights in our lives.
Find some connection with a
child today...

*It is your ancestors who have paved
your way...
thank them...wholeheartedly.
Take a moment and go within...
give thanks...*

It's a new day...
and isn't it beautiful?

Don't look back…don't look forward…
what do you see when you close your eyes?
Experience the moment and treasure it!

It is in darkness that you may see the light, in sadness that you may find joy, and in love that you may release hate… what do you have to release today?

Your family and friends are the solid foundations of your life…
when did you last spend time with them?

If the truth be known,
seek it in your heart...
what is your heart whispering to you?

*Visualize what you fully desire...
and it will be given to you...*

*Divine guidance is looking for you...
have you opened the door?*

Angels say:
"When all is lost in your world…
you still have us…no matter what!"

*Do not judge others…
even if they have wronged you…*

Don't forget the little creatures…
treat them well…
they are all equal in our Universe…

Angels say:
"Take a walk today...
and spend some time with us..."

Worry is "only" affecting your health…
hmm, is that all?
Let go and breathe, there is only love…

Breathe in love, breathe out hate…
breathe in joy, breathe out sorrow…
breathe in peace, breathe out pain….
breathe and continue your mantra…

Do not judge others…
even if you assume you have walked in their shoes…

There's no value in a name, or a title,
without having value in one's heart…

Angels say:
"Call on us day or night…
we don't have time on our plane…"

Seek peace within yourself...
you are your own best friend...

Nature is the most beautiful wonderment…
when was the last time you stopped to smell the roses?

It is not for you to live others' lives…
but to give them a hand
and guide them…

Be still my child...there is no rush...

When you seek outside,
you become lost…
when you seek inside,
you are found…

The gentle clouds that drift by....
are only moments in time...
it is the deep blue sky that remains...
what are your clouds in your life?

Angels say:
"We honor you for who you are…
feel this within your soul
and honor yourself…"

Rejuvenate...
for today is your day of rest...

The ripple affect of doing something for yourself always affects others…

There's always an ending to each story...
how do you want to finish yours?

*Fear is only a concept,
an illusion in your mind…
are you going to give your power
to something that doesn't exist?*

What is it you're searching for?
Does it include love?

Angels say:
"We are your choir...
when your heart sings..."

When your body becomes tired...
listen to it...
many more times than not...
it is signaling for rest...

Don't punish yourself in moments
you're down…
for those are the times you can reach
the top…

Take a break…you deserve it!

Let go of the heavy weight you've been
dragging around…
you don't need it anymore…

Angels say:
"Peace be in your heart…
if not, let us gift it to you…"

Close your eyes... find heaven within...
and take yourself there...

Give something of yourself today...
and watch yourself bloom...

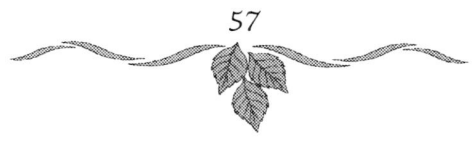

The file cabinet is full...
time to clear the files...

You know you have succeeded when
you have walked a milestone…
and your feet are torn…
now get up and start jogging…

Angels say:
"Be kind to yourself…we are…"

You deserve every ounce that life has to offer.
Believe this for just a second…
and it will be so…

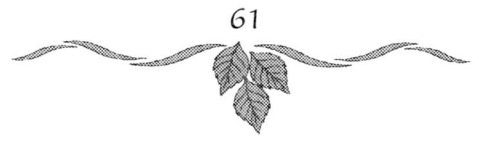

It's not in the way you see things,
but in the way they feel...
acknowledge your heart and follow it...

Let your inner child shine…
play hide and seek…
but let it seek more than hide…

When you rush you lose sight
of the beautiful world around you…
slow down and soak life in…

Breathe…

Angels say:
"Do not be sad our beautiful child...
we are always with you...
feel our presence...
we are keeping you warm and safe..."

It may take work to create peace
within…
but isn't it worth it?
Take a moment and be still…

It's the little things we do that make
the world go 'round...
and the big things that allow us
to stand tall...
where do you stand with both today?

What are your thoughts in this moment? Contemplate...

Your soul should be standing on a mountain high!
If not, what will it take to get you there?

Angels say:
"You are never alone…know that we are by your side…waiting patiently for you to ask for our help…"

Whispers in the wind
softly acknowledge the treasures
within your heart, your soul...
what are they saying?

When you touch another one's soul...
you soar...

When you're in emotional pain...
be humbled by it...
for this is your chance to learn...

To experience the new, is to live...
to avoid it, is to fade...

When sorrow cries,
will you know what you're grateful for?

*It's just another step in life.
Take it! Live a little…*

What did you wake up to today?
The past, which is gone?
The future, which hasn't come?
Or the present...
being in the moment...NOW?

Angels say:
"We know how you feel…we carry all
your emotions, heavy and light…you
are never alone…"

The sun, the moon, and the stars all
come out daily to greet you…
you are one with the Universe…
take a moment to be thankful…

*You know the answer is within…
be still…what does it say?*

What are you grateful for?

Angels say:
"List your burdens on paper…we will
help you work them out…"

Gaze into your past…
are there any regrets?
If so, heal and let them go…renew…

Money is only a utensil…
let go of the need,
for you are already taken care of…

Angels say:
"As high as the tallest peak, as deep as the bluest ocean, as vast as the Universe, that is how much we love you... you are safe and protected..."

Have you wondered lately?
Take a moment and do so…
live here and now…

A cluttered mind leaves no room for peace…
what do you have to clean out today?

Do yourself a favor...
slow down and take a break!

You are already empowered to know
the answers...
have you been listening?

Your body is the only "real" vehicle
you have…
let it know you are grateful for every
part and every inch of it!

Don't lessen the pain by hiding it...
bring it to the surface and release it
forever...

*It is not in how much others love you…
as in how important it is that you
love yourself…*

Angels say:
"Anchor yourself to us...we'll never let you drown...there's truly no death..."

When you limit yourself
you stop living…
life is limitless…keep striving…
grow…

When a friendship fades,
remember the positive memories…
don't dwell on the unhappiness…
let go and feel honored you
experienced it…

To be in the midst of it all
and be centered in peace…
is to truly live…

Does it really matter what the
argument is all about,
when you may only have today?

It is only in the eye of the storm
that you may truly feel at peace…
and only you who can put yourself
there…

When babies take those first few steps,
they do not stop trying after they fall.
They get up, try and try again…

For in the times you feel blue…
    find your inner beauty
    and paint a rainbow…

Dawn's early morning dew dissipates…
as you begin to awaken and shine…
let the Sun shine in…

Angels say:
"We stretch our arms out wide…let us comfort you and love you…we are honored to have you in our presence…honor yourself…"

It is important to allow others to be who they are…
it is their path…their highway.
You may very much be a part of their road…
but don't be their roadblock…

Love is the pure essence of reality…
fear is ego-based illusion…
which do you choose in your life?

It's OK when it's not okay,
because it always ends up being OK
anyway…

Stop plucking your petals…
you are in full bloom…

If you wonder what your
future entails…
think of it as a dream…
coming to fruition…

*The remaining steps in life begin now...
are you going to walk backward
or forward with grace?*

It is in another's eyes that you may see
your own true beauty...
how do you see yourself?

In the quiet moments of the hour…
ask yourself…who am I really?

The I Am of who you truly are
is deep down within your soul…
bring it to the surface and let it
breathe…

To dream is to allow possibilities to exist…
and move them into fruition…

Imagine for a moment looking into a starry night sky…gazing at the vastness of the Universe…this spark of greatness is what already exists within you, if you only allow it to shine…

Like a duck paddling along in life…
you always have a choice to swim
or fly…
what do you choose for yourself today?

Love is only a spelling, a four-letter
word in the dictionary…
but to feel it as an experience
is unlimited…
how do you see or feel love in your life?

When you swim to the other side of the river...
you see things from a different point of view...

Clutter in your mind keeps you from seeing clearly…
free up some space by doing some clearing…

*Stop feeling the regrets of yesterday
or looking for tomorrow's promises…
live today…*

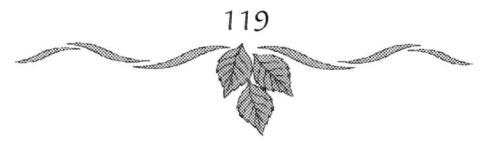

Make the decision now
or lose the opportunity…

Forever exists in your heart,
in your soul…you truly live on…

The uneasiness you're experiencing is your spirit trying to awaken your true essence….
are you going to let it sleep…
or let it rise and shine?

Be careful of being too careful…
for you may never truly live…

It is in complete darkness that you may
find you are the light…
and the power is within you…glow!

When you see it your way…
it's only one way…
turn the direction…
and make it two ways…

Epiphanies are a way of helping you
discover your own inner knowledge…
and awaken the magnificently powerful
being you are…

When the soul whispers quietly,
gently with love…
this is when you truly know the I Am is
here…
are you listening?

What have you done for yourself lately?
Did it include love, peace, or gentleness?
Take time out and treat yourself with kindness…
find something you'd really like to do…

Listen to the words that leave your mouth,
for the slip of the tongue is no accident…
what are they saying to you?

Calm, peace, and tranquility are special
rewards earned after you have learned
to open your heart to true love...

Abundance is alive in your soul…
stop looking outside for it…

Anger is the opposite of peace
and harmony...
it eventually balances itself out.
Be good to yourself...
honor and learn from your feelings,
but do not let them damage you...

Angels say:
"When you try too hard, you lose sight of your true task…let go and let us help you…we all work together to accomplish the same result…relax…"

True beauty begins in the heart...
what do you see within yourself?

The sounds of birds chirping
are the angels' way of acknowledging
their presence…
let your heart sing along…

*When the time is right you will know.
Search within…what is your inner
voice trying to tell you?*

Each day is a wonderful day,
no matter what it looks like…

*It is during the most difficult times
that you understand yourself…*

You will always make it through…

See the light...
be the light and set yourself free...

*Through tears you release, let go…
it's okay to cry…*

There is no such thing as good-bye…
your soul has never left one another's…

The most divine knowledge is…
knowing only love exists…

Angels say:
"We love you no matter what you do…
or where you go…we are one with you
and you will always have us…"

*You have been released;
now spread your wings and fly…*

Kindness is lesson one…
patience is lesson two…
compassion is the test…
love is the reward…

Free will is a gift given to you
by the Omnipotent.
Choose wisely and your rewards will be
tremendous…

It is in the face of sorrow
that you find your greatest strength...

Earth holds many lessons for
your soul…
you will travel many tests of time
and pass…
failure is not an option
and never has been…

Negative energies exist to bring out the
positive ones you have always had.
Do not give power to anything,
but to your true self...
how would you convert your energies?

It is within the treasure chest of your
soul that you will find your jewels…
open it and look inside…

As difficult as things may seem,
eventually they will become easier…
have faith…
take one step at a time
and come off the mountain…

This too shall pass; it always does...

You are a spiritual leader helping souls
to awaken…
don't lose sight of your purpose…

We are all like individual snowflakes:
different from one another, yet upon
melting we blend into the same liquid,
water…

Blind yourself to the truth and you may
never see it the same way again...

*Close your eyes to illusion;
only reality exists…*

The spark in a baby's eyes
allows you to find your own…

Find the answer in your heart…
that's where it lives…

*It's not the pain that matters…
but how you handle the situation
that counts…*

As the clock keeps ticking
and time passes by…inquire…
have you lost or found yourself?

It is the person you have not yet met
whom you may find to be your
best friend…keep your eyes open…

An ailment within your body is the symptom of allowing negative energy in… now gently allow it to leave…

By standing in your own shoes as others cannot...
you will always know yourself better.
Be kind and give them slippers...
and help them understand you...

*The twinkle in your heart is aching to find its way…
follow your desire and shine!*

There is nowhere to look;
you are standing in your soul…

If you choose the fast lane,
you will miss opportunities…
slow down and enjoy the view;
it's right in front of you…

Does it really matter, anyway?

Look within…
you already have the answer…

When you push against the wind,
you struggle…
turn around, let the wind push you,
and fly!

*It is in the smallest of things
that you see the big picture…*

Counting the days that may not exist,
doesn't count...live in the now!

There is a holiday in your heart,
all year 'round...

Each person is a mirror of yourself;
are you happy with what you see?

In each person
you find a spark of yourself...

You are a gift to this World…

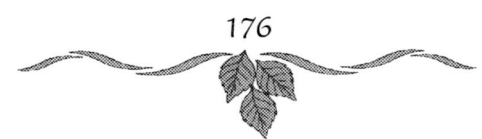

*You equal the whole…
whole equals one…one equals you…
you are the whole of every one…*

*Forgive and experience
your true essence…*

Moderation keeps you in balance…

When you are in an argument,
find the middle ground…

Give of yourself, awaken!

Waiting is only a practice of patience…
truly, time does not exist…

In times when you may feel like drowning,
you always have a choice
to surface and swim to shore…

*It is in your initial gut reaction
wherein lives the truth;
trust it and follow your instinct…*

Heal your heart...heal your soul...

Forgive and feel one of the greatest empowerments of all!

There is no right or wrong,
only lessons of truth and love...

Your power lies in the inner strength of helping others as well as yourself. Learn to balance this and your benefits will be great…

You are a teacher as well as a student…
at any given time you are offering gifts
as well as accepting them…

*When you learn to let go,
you'll break the chains that bind you...*

Guiding yourself to move on
allows you the breathing space
to grow, to bloom…

What you desire is around the corner...
choose your path wisely...

It's in compromising your dignity that
you weaken,
rising above it all that you strengthen…

You have always deserved the best...
accept nothing less...

Abundance blooms within…
begin with faith…

It is only through peace that you will
see the whole picture
and paint love on the canvas…

You are always being assisted,
even when it doesn't feel like it
or you haven't asked…
you are never alone…

Release the grip you have on life
and live a little...

It's when the door is closed
that divine guidance can't come in...
keep the door open...

Your emotions are sailing the
turbulent seas...
ease up on your vessel with peace
and bring your ship to calmer waters...

Don't make a decision while you're
confused.
Wait awhile…
and see it from another angle…

It's in each small step you take,
each lesson you learn
that takes you where you are going
on your journey inward…

Positive and loving perspectives come
from calm and quiet moments…

A new day is dawning, ready to hold
your hand and guide you…
walk with your chin up
and let the sun warm your soul…

*Knowledge is power,
if you use it wisely…*

When change enters your life,
will you know how to handle it?

You are the only one
standing in your way…

It is in judging others
that you belittle yourself…

Be careful if you have a hand in gossip;
it may come back and smack you…

There is no such thing as a secret
in this Universe...

You are always protected…

When something doesn't feel right, stop,
look around, and seek clarity...

Positive and fresh energies are on the horizon…
be patient, relax and enjoy…

*Don't look for it…
let it come to you…*

When you feel misunderstood,
find the strength to forgive and
rise above…

Hide all you want…
eventually you will be found…

You are a light-worker,
here to help others awaken,
to rise and shine…

Life is a merry-go-round,
with many ups and downs…
but it's in how you pace yourself
that determines the ride…

The way you view the World
is a reflection of yourself…

Take a moment to look at the horizon…
what do you see?
And how does it make you feel?

Faith and Hope may not affirm a
guarantee in life,
but they do offer strength and power in
times of need…
they are here to help you move on
when nothing else does…

The physical parts of you
face challenges to test how strong
your soul is …

You are healed…
you are perfect…

The way to understand a situation
is through the eyes of love...

You are immensely loved!

Visualize what you desire…
it's alive, in fruition…

There are options available...
the choice is always yours...
this is God's gift...

Be yourself…always…

Your divine purpose is blooming,
coming to fruition.
Be patient…

Pushing against the tide
will only drown you…
surf the wave instead and
enjoy the ride…

You are coming out of your dream state,
ready to awaken…rise and shine!

Following is as important as leading…
it's not only in the manner of how you decide to follow,
but in how you decide to lead…
one cannot occur without the other…

True independence is a gift you give
to yourself,
through many accomplishments…

It is when you have accepted the love of God that you will truly feel secure…

It's time for a healthy change in your life; ask your Angels to help you…

What is it your heart is saying?

Personal growth comes from education,
by learning the lessons…

Compassion lives in seeing true colors in another and kindly accepting the rainbow…

By giving and receiving equally,
you help balance the Universe…

Being conscious allows you to live
in the present moment…

Entrapments are figments of the ego,
creations of the mind…
Free yourself, breathe!

Determination of the soul
keeps you alive...

Plant the seed, water it properly,
and it will bloom…

Fear allows you to die...
risk encourages you to live...

No need to rush,
if you live in the present moment…
NOW!

It is when the mask is removed that
illusion fades and reality brightens…

Shift your energy,
change your circumstance…

Survival of the fittest is purely spiritual, not physical; only true reality exists…

The mirror effect of judging others
is always a boomerang of your own…

Calmness amidst crisis
is one of the true tests of the soul…

*Detaching yourself from negativity
empowers you…*

After exhausting all avenues,
accepting the "as is" in life with
sincerity proves authentic power…

Running away is a weakness,
facing it the strength…

*Negative energies are heavy,
positive energies light.
It's always your choice to put yourself
down or bring yourself up…*

You are already purely perfect;
see this from a wholesome point of view
as you grow spiritually…

A bumpy road is only a detour while
you slowly return to the highway…

We are all like dominos,
each equally the same in structure
yet individually different,
here to lean on one another…

Negative emotions, internal or external,
are triggers crying out from your soul…
evaluate and heal…

If a part of you wants to sigh, ignore…
if the whole of you needs to breathe,
pay attention…

Repressing is weakness;
expressing is strength...

Chasing money will only get you the loss of your soul…
seek love instead and you will be fulfilled…

Imagine slowly walking through a forest, coming to a clearing, opening your mind, and hearing your answer…

Each lesson you learn is a step closer to graduation.
Study well and enjoy the class…

You may not be able to change everyone and everything around you, but you can certainly shift your energies and change your world…

No matter where you go
or how you get there,
you are always being watched over
and cared for…

Your choices in life always include
either love or fear, but not both...
they cannot exist at the same time...

Once you let go of doubt,
trust remains…

Pain is an emotion trying to awaken the part of you that does not feel love...

Fatigue is your body's cry
for replenishing positive energies…

*Spirituality is the fruit of the soul…
God is the seed…*

Heartache is the physical condition
of fear, the absence of love…

Unlocking the bolt to your heart…
opens the door to your home…

Earth is your temporary home;
make the best of it…

*Stop fighting the battle...
victory has reigned!*

Your spiritual journey
is always an adventure…

Every physical ailment
has an emotional attachment;
finding the root
will cure the problem…

Help others feel good;
allow them to teach you something…

An unhealthy attitude is the loss of self,
healthy when it's found…

Health is being kind to your body,
mind, and soul…

Life's compass is in your heart;
which direction is it guiding you?
Navigate and it will lead you…

God bless my food
and raise its vibration…

You never get away with anything negative in life, because in the end you're only harming yourself…

What may seem normal or right to you
may not to another, and vice versa...
do not pass judgment...

Help the souls who feel unworthy
of helping themselves...

Hurdles, emotional or physical, are only temporary; eventually you must leap to the other side…

Second chances are the Universe's way
of testing your faith...

You can let go…anytime now…

Life is a maze, of your creation…

The more you focus on materialism,
the less of yourself you become…

Always keep your dignity…

The beauty and awe of a sunrise and sunset are only tiny glimpses of how beautiful your eternal soul is...

If you keep allowing worry to bother you, ego keeps winning and taking your power…

Accompany the reality of love,
not the illusion of ego,
as your best friend…

Follow through with your
commitments...

If a situation saddens you,
step back and see it from
a brighter side…

The first step to living, is breathing…

Close your eyes, take a deep breath, softly exhale, and slowly open your eyes...

Be aware of how you treat the next person you meet.
This stranger might just become your best friend…

*What the gift is that you receive
is not as important
as how you react to it…*

Pay attention to others' lessons;
you might just learn from them ...

Miracles come from believing…

The remedy for a broken heart
is a stained-glass of forgiveness...

Follow your passion
and it will lead you...

Continue each step, one by one...

Do what feels natural…

Recognition is the first step
to healing...

Painting a mural of acceptance is the art
of learning to love yourself...

Security comes from fully trusting the Universe...

Prayer is the key to unlocking doors…

You are the interior designer
of your life…
what patterns do you plan to use?

Eat well...

Bring your passion to the surface…

Knocking yourself down,
will not help you reach the top…

Is there a song in your heart…singing?

Allow the new to come in…

Once you let the fear of death go,
you awaken and begin to live...

Experience your anger…
then release it with love…

Courage allows you to live life
to the fullest...

Detaching from your feelings
is a form of alienation...
honoring them is accepting yourself...

Peace...